He

aCtIve
maths

Pupil Book 4
Fractions

Authors: Peter Gorrie, Lynda Keith, Lynne McClure, Amy Sinclair

How to use this book

Contents

Instructions look like this. Always read these carefully before starting.

These are Rocket activities. Ask your teacher if you need to do these questions.

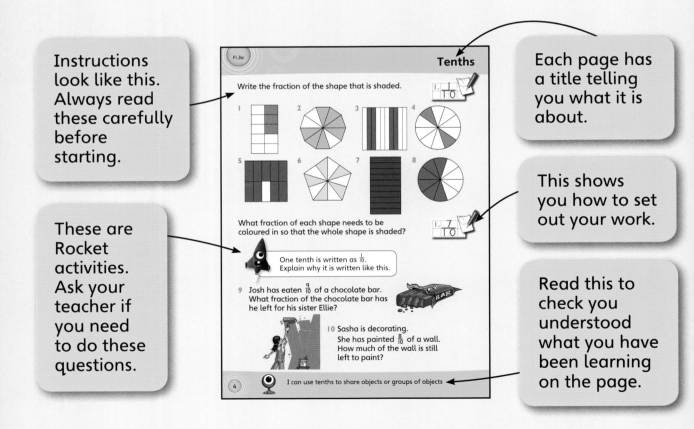

Each page has a title telling you what it is about.

This shows you how to set out your work.

Read this to check you understood what you have been learning on the page.

Tenths

1 Which of the shapes show tenths?

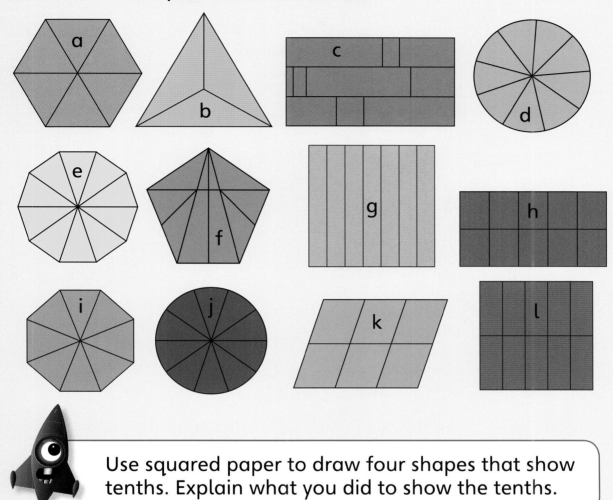

Use squared paper to draw four shapes that show tenths. Explain what you did to show the tenths.

What can you do to these shapes to make them show tenths?

2

3

  I can recognise shapes that are divided into tenths

Tenths

Write the fraction of the shape that is shaded.

1. $\frac{3}{10}$

1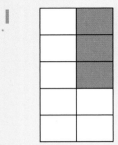

2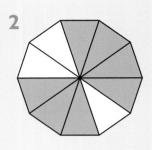

3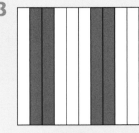

4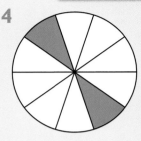

5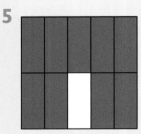

6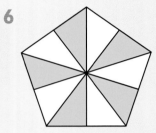

7

8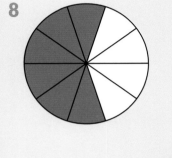

What fraction of each shape needs to be coloured in so that the whole shape is shaded?

1. $\frac{7}{10}$

One tenth is written as $\frac{1}{10}$.
Explain why it is written like this.

9 Josh has eaten $\frac{9}{10}$ of a chocolate bar.
What fraction of the chocolate bar has
he left for his sister Ellie?

10 Sasha is decorating.
She has painted $\frac{8}{10}$ of a wall.
How much of the wall is still
left to paint?

I can use tenths to share objects or groups of objects

Tenths

Find $\frac{1}{10}$ of the cakes on the tray.

1. $\frac{1}{10}$ of 20 = 2

1

2

3

4

5

6

 Is it possible to find a tenth of your class?
If not, why not?

Copy and complete.

7 $\frac{1}{10}$ of 60 = ☐   8 $\frac{1}{10}$ of 80 = ☐   9 $\frac{1}{10}$ of 100 = ☐

10 $\frac{1}{10}$ of 130 = ☐   11 $\frac{1}{10}$ of 200 = ☐   12 $\frac{1}{10}$ of 170 = ☐

13 $\frac{1}{10}$ of 440 = ☐   14 $\frac{1}{10}$ of 320 = ☐   15 $\frac{1}{10}$ of 510 = ☐

I can find tenths of a number of objects

2 of the cubes are blue.
$\frac{1}{10}$ of the cubes are blue.
There are 20 cubes altogether.

How many cubes are there altogether if $\frac{1}{10}$ is:

1 4 cubes	2 7 cubes	3 8 cubes	4 12 cubes
5 9 cubes	6 13 cubes	7 21 cubes	8 32 cubes

A decade is 10 years. 1 year is a tenth of a decade. 'Dec' means 10. What other words do you know with 'dec' in? What do they mean?

Copy and complete, using the correct symbol.

9. $\frac{1}{2}$ of 20 > $\frac{1}{10}$ of 50

9   $\frac{1}{2}$ of 20 [ ] $\frac{1}{10}$ of 50

10   $\frac{1}{2}$ of 50 [ ] $\frac{1}{10}$ of 40

11   $\frac{1}{2}$ of 20 [ ] $\frac{1}{10}$ of 100

12   $\frac{1}{2}$ of 30 [ ] $\frac{1}{10}$ of 400

13 Finn asks Kaya if she would rather have $\frac{1}{10}$ of £240 or $\frac{1}{2}$ of £46.
What should Kaya say?

 I can find a tenth of a number

Tenths on a number line

What number is each arrow pointing to?

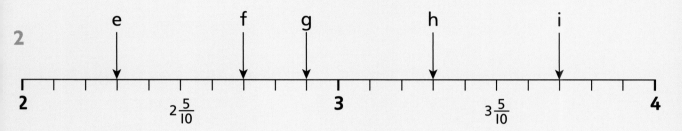

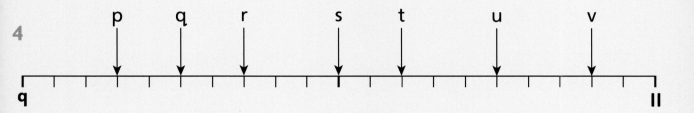

Copy the number line and mark these numbers on it.

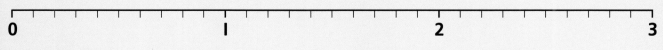

5 $\frac{3}{10}$ 6 $\frac{7}{10}$ 7 $2\frac{1}{10}$ 8 $1\frac{6}{10}$

9 $1\frac{4}{10}$ 10 $2\frac{4}{10}$ 11 $\frac{1}{2}$ 12 $2\frac{1}{2}$

 I can count in tenths and record this on a number line

7

Writing tenths

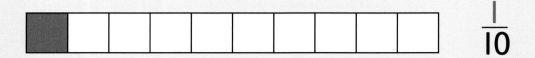

$\dfrac{1}{10}$

One tenth is I part of a **whole** object that is divided into
10 equal parts.

1   Draw a picture and write a sentence for seven tenths.

2   Gabby and her brother Max are
on a journey that is 200 km long.
They have gone $\frac{2}{10}$ of the way.
How far have they gone?

 Gabby draws a picture to show Max
where they are in their journey.
Draw Gabby's picture.

3   What fraction of the
journey is still to go?

4   How many kilometres to go
to complete the journey?

5   What fraction of
the petrol is left
in the fuel tank?

  I can use tenths to do calculations

Fifths

1 **Which of the shapes show fifths?**

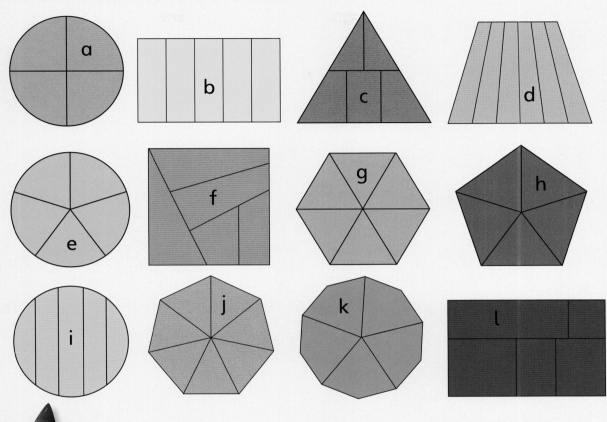

Use squared paper to draw four shapes that show fifths. Explain what you did to show the fifths.

What can you do to these shapes to make them show fifths?

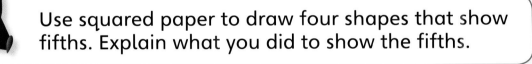

2

3

I can recognise shapes that are divided into fifths

9

Fifths

Write the fraction of red buttons.

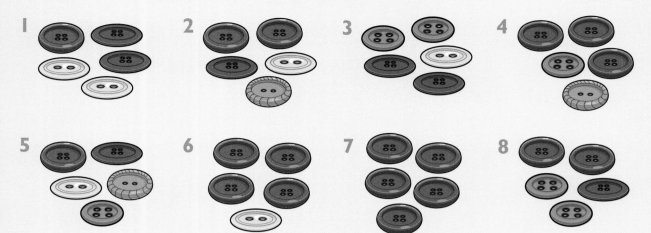

Choose some other colours to count. Write the fractions.

Write the fraction of clowns that:

9   are happy

10 are wearing glasses

11 have a blue nose

12 are wearing a hat

13 are wearing a bow tie

14 have a red nose and are sad

15 are wearing a hat and are happy

16 are wearing a hat and a bow tie

  I can find fifths of a number of objects

Fifths and tenths

4 of the cubes are blue.
$\frac{1}{5}$ of the cubes are blue.
There are 20 cubes altogether.

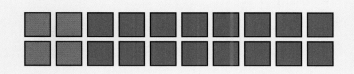

How many cubes are there altogether if $\frac{1}{5}$ is:

1	5 cubes	2	3 cubes	3	8 cubes	4	6 cubes
5	9 cubes	6	17 cubes	7	10 cubes	8	7 cubes

Use 5 red and 5 yellow counters.
Explore how you can show fractions
of red counters in fifths. Record each
one with a picture and a fraction.

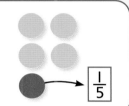

Copy and complete,
using the correct symbol.

9. $\frac{1}{10}$ of 100 > $\frac{1}{5}$ of 40

9   $\frac{1}{10}$ of 100   ☐ $\frac{1}{5}$ of 40

10   $\frac{1}{10}$ of 40   ☐ $\frac{1}{5}$ of 50

11   $\frac{1}{5}$ of 30   ☐ $\frac{1}{10}$ of 100

12   $\frac{1}{10}$ of 20   ☐ $\frac{1}{5}$ of 10

13 Sol asks Laila if she would rather
have $\frac{1}{10}$ of £80 or $\frac{1}{5}$ of £40.
What should Laila say?

I can find a fifth and a tenth of a number

Fifths

Draw a picture to help you find your answers.

1   There are 30 children in the class.
    $\frac{1}{5}$ of the children have a pet dog.
    How many children have a pet dog?

2   As well as the children with pet dogs,
    $\frac{1}{5}$ of the children have a cat and $\frac{1}{5}$ of
    the children have a goldfish.
    The rest of the class do not have any pets.
    What fraction of the class do not have a pet?
    How many children is that?

3   Mica has 50 stickers. Esme has a fifth more.
    How many stickers does Esme have?

4   The school football team played 20 games.
    They lost one fifth of the games.
    How many games did they win?

Use words and pictures to describe everything you know about fifths. Here are some words you could use:

equal   denominator
                            numerator
$\frac{1}{5}$ fifth
                fraction   whole

I can use fifths to do calculations

Fifths on a number line

What number is each arrow pointing to?

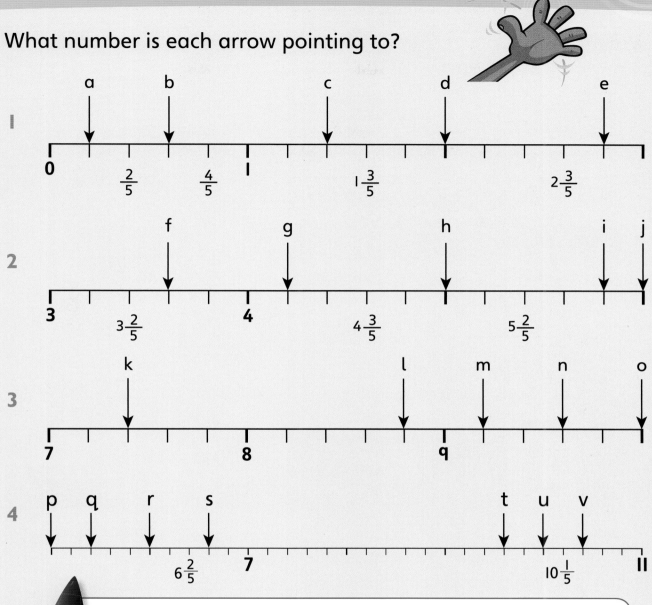

Copy and complete this number line, marking in all the fifths.

How many fifths are there between 0 and 12?
How many fifths would there be if the number line was from 0 to 100? How do you know?

 I can count in fifths and record this on a number line

13

Hundredths

Write the fraction of the
coloured part of each square.

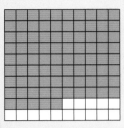

1. $\dfrac{35}{100}$

1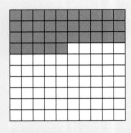

2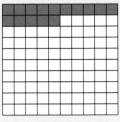

3

4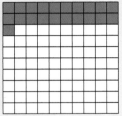

5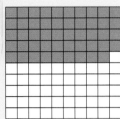

6

7   Which picture shows 75 hundredths?

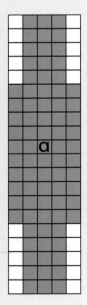

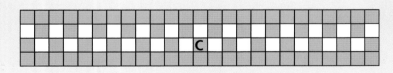

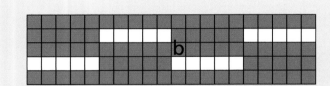

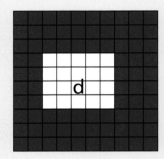

a

b

c

d

Use squared paper to draw some more shapes
that show 75 hundredths.

   I can identify hundredths of a shape

Hundredths

What fraction of each square is shaded? Is not shaded?

1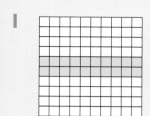

2

3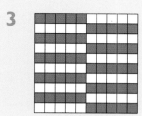

4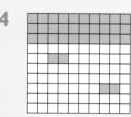

5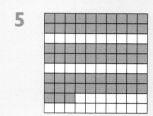

6

7

8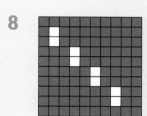

9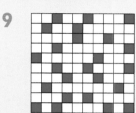

10 How many hundredths are there in a whole square?

11 How many hundredths are there in a half of the square?

What household items do you know that use hundredths?

Copy and complete, using the correct symbol.

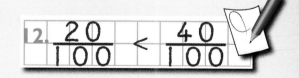
12. $\dfrac{20}{100} < \dfrac{40}{100}$

12 $\dfrac{20}{100}$ ☐ $\dfrac{40}{100}$ 13 $\dfrac{63}{100}$ ☐ $\dfrac{34}{100}$

14 $\dfrac{24}{100}$ ☐ $\dfrac{20}{100}$ 15 I whole ☐ $\dfrac{100}{100}$

16 $\dfrac{39}{100}$ ☐ $\dfrac{75}{100}$ 17 $\dfrac{1}{2}$ ☐ $\dfrac{50}{100}$

 I can identify hundredths of a shape and compare hundredths

Comparing fractions

I whole			
$\frac{1}{2}$		$\frac{1}{2}$	
$\frac{1}{4}$	$\frac{1}{4}$	$\frac{1}{4}$	$\frac{1}{4}$

Which is bigger?

1 $\frac{1}{2}$ or $\frac{1}{4}$ **2** $\frac{3}{4}$ or $\frac{1}{2}$

3 $\frac{3}{4}$ or I whole   **4** $\frac{2}{4}$ or $\frac{1}{2}$

5 What number does each letter represent?

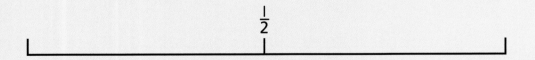

Write five fractions statements about halves and quarters. Use the symbols <, > and =.

I can use a fraction wall to identify and compare halves and quarters

Comparing fractions

I whole									
$\frac{1}{2}$					$\frac{1}{2}$				
$\frac{1}{5}$		$\frac{1}{5}$		$\frac{1}{5}$		$\frac{1}{5}$		$\frac{1}{5}$	
$\frac{1}{10}$	$\frac{1}{10}$	$\frac{1}{10}$	$\frac{1}{10}$	$\frac{1}{10}$	$\frac{1}{10}$	$\frac{1}{10}$	$\frac{1}{10}$	$\frac{1}{10}$	$\frac{1}{10}$

Which is bigger?

1 $\frac{1}{10}$ or $\frac{1}{5}$ **2** $\frac{2}{5}$ or $\frac{1}{2}$ **3** $\frac{6}{10}$ or $\frac{1}{2}$

4 $\frac{3}{5}$ or $\frac{7}{10}$ **5** $\frac{9}{10}$ or I whole

Copy and complete,
using the correct symbol.

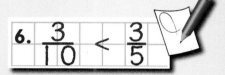

6. $\frac{3}{10} < \frac{3}{5}$

6 $\frac{3}{10}$ ☐ $\frac{3}{5}$ **7** $\frac{1}{2}$ ☐ $\frac{3}{5}$

8 $\frac{4}{5}$ ☐ $\frac{8}{10}$ **9** $\frac{7}{10}$ ☐ $\frac{4}{5}$

10 I whole ☐ $\frac{2}{2}$

Write the fractions in order, from largest to smallest.

11 $\frac{1}{5}$ $\frac{1}{10}$ $\frac{1}{2}$ **12** $\frac{2}{10}$ $\frac{1}{2}$ $\frac{3}{5}$

13 $\frac{4}{5}$ $\frac{2}{10}$ $\frac{1}{2}$ **14** I whole $\frac{2}{10}$ $\frac{4}{5}$

Write these fractions in order, from smallest to largest. What do you notice?

$\frac{1}{2}$ $\frac{6}{10}$ $\frac{1}{5}$ $\frac{3}{5}$ $\frac{2}{10}$ $\frac{5}{10}$

Comparing fractions

1 **What number does each letter represent?**

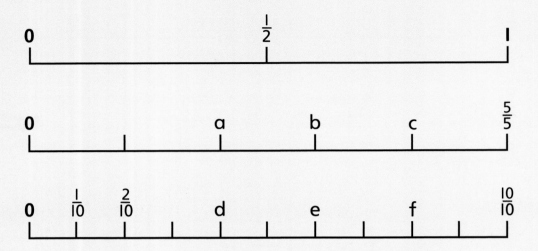

2 Write a fraction that is bigger than $\frac{6}{10}$ but smaller than $\frac{4}{5}$.

3 Write a fraction that is smaller than $\frac{1}{2}$ but bigger than $\frac{2}{10}$.

Write these fractions in order, from smallest to largest.

4 $\frac{1}{2}$ $\frac{1}{10}$ $\frac{1}{5}$ **5** $\frac{3}{5}$ $\frac{1}{5}$ $\frac{4}{10}$ $\frac{7}{10}$

Write five fractions statements about fifths, tenths and halves, using the = symbol.

I can compare halves, fifths and tenths

Ordering fractions

Write the slices of pizzas as fractions,
using <, > or =.

1. $\frac{1}{2} > \frac{1}{5}$

1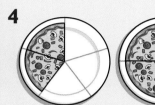

2

3

4

5

6

 How much pizza has been eaten on each plate?

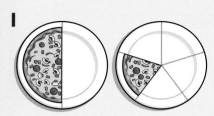

I whole			
$\frac{1}{2}$		$\frac{1}{2}$	
$\frac{1}{4}$	$\frac{1}{4}$	$\frac{1}{4}$	$\frac{1}{4}$

$\frac{1}{5}$ $\frac{1}{5}$ $\frac{1}{5}$ $\frac{1}{5}$ $\frac{1}{5}$

$\frac{1}{10}$ $\frac{1}{10}$ $\frac{1}{10}$ $\frac{1}{10}$ $\frac{1}{10}$ $\frac{1}{10}$ $\frac{1}{10}$ $\frac{1}{10}$ $\frac{1}{10}$ $\frac{1}{10}$

Write these fractions in order,
from smallest to largest.

7 $\frac{1}{5}$ $\frac{1}{10}$ $\frac{1}{2}$

8 $\frac{1}{5}$ $\frac{1}{4}$ $\frac{1}{10}$

9 $\frac{1}{2}$ $\frac{1}{10}$ $\frac{1}{4}$ $\frac{1}{5}$

10 $\frac{3}{5}$ $\frac{2}{4}$ $\frac{9}{10}$

11 Choose five fractions for a partner to order, from largest
to smallest. Check their answer.

I can compare and order simple fractions

Comparing fractions

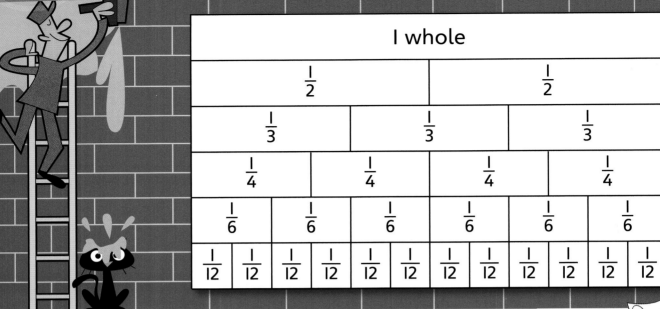

I whole											
$\frac{1}{2}$						$\frac{1}{2}$					
$\frac{1}{3}$				$\frac{1}{3}$				$\frac{1}{3}$			
$\frac{1}{4}$			$\frac{1}{4}$			$\frac{1}{4}$			$\frac{1}{4}$		
$\frac{1}{6}$		$\frac{1}{6}$		$\frac{1}{6}$		$\frac{1}{6}$		$\frac{1}{6}$		$\frac{1}{6}$	
$\frac{1}{12}$	$\frac{1}{12}$	$\frac{1}{12}$	$\frac{1}{12}$	$\frac{1}{12}$	$\frac{1}{12}$	$\frac{1}{12}$	$\frac{1}{12}$	$\frac{1}{12}$	$\frac{1}{12}$	$\frac{1}{12}$	$\frac{1}{12}$

Copy and write the missing numbers.

1. $\frac{1}{2} = \frac{2}{4}$

1. $\frac{1}{2} = \frac{\boxed{}}{4}$

2. $\frac{1}{3} = \frac{\boxed{}}{6}$

3. $\frac{2}{3} = \frac{\boxed{}}{6}$

4. $\frac{6}{6} = \frac{\boxed{}}{3}$

5. $\frac{1}{2} = \frac{3}{\boxed{}}$

6. $\frac{3}{4} = \frac{\boxed{}}{12}$

7. $\frac{3}{12} = \frac{1}{\boxed{}}$

8. $\frac{4}{12} = \frac{1}{\boxed{}}$

9. $\frac{8}{12} = \frac{\boxed{}}{3}$

Draw a fractions wall for I whole, halves, fifths and tenths. Write some statements for the fractions on your fractions board, for example $\frac{2}{5} = \frac{4}{10}$.

10 Mena has to give away 3 out of 6 marbles.
Becky has to give away 4 out of her 8 marbles.
Are they giving away the same fraction?

I can compare simple fractions

Comparing fractions

Write the uneaten pizzas as fractions, using <.

1. $\dfrac{1}{3} < \dfrac{1}{2}$

1

2

3

4

5

6

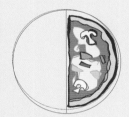   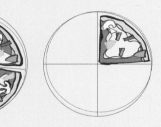 

Which plate has the most pizza to eat? Which plate has the least pizza to eat? How do you know?

Write <, > or = between each pair.

$\frac{1}{2}$		$\frac{1}{2}$	
$\frac{1}{3}$		$\frac{1}{3}$	$\frac{1}{3}$
$\frac{1}{4}$	$\frac{1}{4}$	$\frac{1}{4}$	$\frac{1}{4}$

$\frac{1}{3}$		$\frac{1}{3}$		$\frac{1}{3}$	
$\frac{1}{6}$	$\frac{1}{6}$	$\frac{1}{6}$	$\frac{1}{6}$	$\frac{1}{6}$	$\frac{1}{6}$
$\frac{1}{12}$	$\frac{1}{12}$	$\frac{1}{12}$	$\frac{1}{12}$	$\frac{1}{12}$	$\frac{1}{12}$	$\frac{1}{12}$	$\frac{1}{12}$	$\frac{1}{12}$	$\frac{1}{12}$	$\frac{1}{12}$	$\frac{1}{12}$

7 $\dfrac{1}{2}$ $\dfrac{2}{3}$

8 $\dfrac{1}{3}$ $\dfrac{1}{4}$

9 $\dfrac{2}{3}$ $\dfrac{3}{4}$

10 $\dfrac{2}{4}$ $\dfrac{1}{2}$

11 $\dfrac{1}{4}$ $\dfrac{1}{2}$

12 $\dfrac{2}{3}$ $\dfrac{2}{4}$

13 $\dfrac{1}{3}$ $\dfrac{5}{12}$

14 $\dfrac{7}{12}$ $\dfrac{2}{3}$

15 $\dfrac{5}{6}$ $\dfrac{2}{3}$

16 $\dfrac{1}{6}$ $\dfrac{1}{3}$

17 $\dfrac{3}{6}$ $\dfrac{6}{12}$

18 $\dfrac{5}{6}$ $\dfrac{11}{12}$

I can compare simple fractions

Ordering fractions

Use the fraction wall to help you write each
set of fractions in order, smallest to largest.

1. $\frac{1}{5}$, $\frac{1}{3}$...

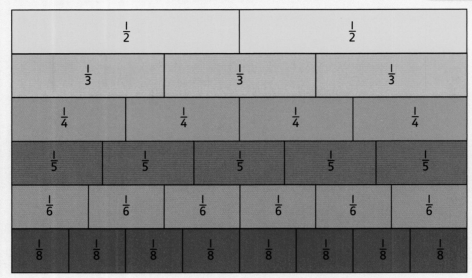

$\frac{1}{2}$			$\frac{1}{2}$		

$\frac{1}{3}$ $\frac{1}{3}$ $\frac{1}{3}$

$\frac{1}{4}$ $\frac{1}{4}$ $\frac{1}{4}$ $\frac{1}{4}$

$\frac{1}{5}$ $\frac{1}{5}$ $\frac{1}{5}$ $\frac{1}{5}$ $\frac{1}{5}$

$\frac{1}{6}$ $\frac{1}{6}$ $\frac{1}{6}$ $\frac{1}{6}$ $\frac{1}{6}$ $\frac{1}{6}$

$\frac{1}{8}$ $\frac{1}{8}$ $\frac{1}{8}$ $\frac{1}{8}$ $\frac{1}{8}$ $\frac{1}{8}$ $\frac{1}{8}$ $\frac{1}{8}$

1 $\frac{1}{3}$, $\frac{2}{4}$, $\frac{1}{5}$, $\frac{2}{3}$, $\frac{3}{5}$

2 $\frac{4}{5}$, $\frac{1}{3}$, $\frac{1}{4}$, $\frac{2}{5}$, $\frac{2}{4}$

3 $\frac{3}{6}$, $\frac{2}{8}$, $\frac{1}{3}$, $\frac{3}{4}$, $\frac{7}{8}$

4 $\frac{4}{5}$, $\frac{3}{4}$, $\frac{1}{2}$, $\frac{1}{4}$, $\frac{2}{5}$

5 $\frac{3}{4}$, $\frac{2}{3}$, $\frac{5}{6}$, $\frac{3}{8}$, $\frac{1}{6}$

6 $\frac{5}{8}$, $\frac{2}{3}$, $\frac{1}{8}$, $\frac{2}{4}$, $\frac{3}{8}$

7 $\frac{3}{4}$, $\frac{2}{3}$, $\frac{3}{5}$, $\frac{1}{2}$, $\frac{2}{5}$

8 $\frac{1}{8}$, $\frac{5}{8}$, $\frac{2}{3}$, $\frac{1}{3}$, $\frac{2}{4}$

9 $\frac{1}{6}$, $\frac{3}{4}$, $\frac{7}{8}$, $\frac{1}{3}$, $\frac{4}{5}$

10 Write some fractions between $\frac{1}{2}$ and $\frac{3}{4}$.

Use these cards: 1 2 3 4 5 6

Make pairs of fractions, one smaller than
the other: $<$

$\frac{1}{6} < \frac{2}{5}$

How many pairs can you make?
How many equal pairs can you make?

I can compare and order simple fractions

Ordering fractions

For each set of candles, write the fraction of red candles.

1

2

3

4

5

6

7

8

9

Write the fraction of yellow candles in each set. Then write these fractions in order from largest to smallest.

Use up to 6 counters, which can be red or yellow.

Explore how many different fractions of red counters you can show. Record each one with a picture and a fraction. What are the largest and smallest fractions that you can find?

$\frac{5}{6}$ $\frac{1}{4}$ $\frac{2}{5}$

Comparing fractions

I am a fraction. Guess who I am.

1 My bottom number is 4. I am less than $\frac{1}{3}$.

2 My top number is 3. I am more than $\frac{2}{3}$.

3 My top and bottom numbers have a total of 9. I am the same size as $\frac{1}{2}$.

4 My bottom number is double my top number and they have a total of 12.

5 My top number is 2 less than my bottom number. I am the same size as $\frac{3}{4}$.

6 My top number is 1. I am between $\frac{1}{4}$ and $\frac{1}{2}$.

 Invent your own 'Guess who I am' fraction clues.

Write the missing numbers. Some may have more than one answer.

7 $\frac{\Box}{5} < \frac{1}{2}$ **8** $\frac{\Box}{8} < \frac{3}{4}$ **9** $\frac{\Box}{3} < \frac{1}{2}$ **10** $\frac{\Box}{4} < \frac{5}{8}$

11 $\frac{1}{2} < \frac{\Box}{6}$ **12** $\frac{2}{3} = \frac{\Box}{6}$ **13** $\frac{\Box}{8} > \frac{1}{2}$ **14** $\frac{3}{5} > \frac{\Box}{4}$

15 $\frac{\Box}{8} < \frac{1}{4}$ **16** $\frac{5}{6} > \frac{\Box}{3}$ **17** $\frac{8}{8} = \frac{\Box}{4}$ **18** $1 = \frac{\Box}{3}$

I can compare and order fractions